Buzzing Aro

Buzzing Around Tax Facts With Be's

By India Roberts

Buzzing Around Tax Facts With Be's

©2016 India Roberts

All Rights Reserved

ISBN

1523359110

No part of the contents of this work may be reproduced, stored in a retrieval system or retransmitted in any form without the permission of the author.

Buzzing Around Tax Facts With Be's

Dedicated To:

Be's Professional Services, LLC is dedicated to my mother. My mother Bobbie E. Fisher is one of the sweeties, humbling, loving, non-judging and trust worthy people you could ever meet. Her finger print in this world is powerful. Our goal at Be's Professional Services is to impact and serve as many individuals and business as we can.

Buzzing Around Tax Facts With Be's

Special Thanks To:

I would like to first thank God for all the blessings and strength that he has given me and to my loving children and family, DeMonte', Hazel and Hannah Roberts who has been there for me.

Buzzing Around Tax Facts With Be's

Connect With Me:

https://www.facebook.com/taxseasonready

https://www.linkedin.com/in/besproservices

https://twitter.com/besproservices

Buzzing Around Tax Facts With Be's

Table of Contents

Table of Contents 6

Tax Season Has Started!!! 9

Your Bill of Rights as a Taxpayer! 16

2015 Tax Law Updates 17

Chapter One 24

What You Need to Know About IRS and Health Care 24

Information That the Health Coverage Providers Reported to the IRS 24

FYI--Affordable Care Act – Individuals 26

The Individual Shared Responsibility Provision 27

Chapter Two 29

Employers and the IRS 29

ACA Information for Employers Counting Full-time and Full-time Equivalent Employees 29

A.C.A. and Employers Understanding Affordable and Minimum Value Coverage 31

Chapter Three 33

How Getting Married/ Divorced Can Affect Your Taxes 33

Getting Married Can Affect Your Premium Tax Credit 33

Key Tax Tips for Divorce or Separation 35

Chapter Four 38

How to Get Tax Credits For Childcare and Education 38

Get Credit for Child and Dependent Care This Summer 38

Buzzing Around Tax Facts With Be's

Education Tax Credits 41

Chapter Five 43

Moving or Selling Your Home and the IRS 43

Moving Can Affect Your Premium Tax Credit 43

Here Are Ten Tax Facts To Know If You Sell Your Home!! 45

Chapter Six 47

Tips/Facts You Should Know When Filling an Amended Return 47

Tax Tips about Filing an Amended Tax Return 47

Nine Facts on Filing an Amended Return 49

Chapter Seven 51

Tips You Should Know When Giving To Charity 51

501(c) (3) Exemption Requirements 51

    Tips for Year-End Gifts to Charity 53

Tips on Travel While Giving Your Services to Charity 55

IRS.... Tax Guidance Related to Ebola Outbreak in Guinea, Liberia and Sierra Leone 58

Chapter Eight 60

Tax Breaks and Benefits for Military 60

    Tax Benefits for Members of the Armed Forces 60

Tips about Tax Breaks for the Military 63

Chapter Nine 66

Running Your Own Business to Looking For a Job Tax Tips 66

Five Basic Tax Tips for New Businesses 66

7

Buzzing Around Tax Facts With Be's

Job Hunting Expenses 69
New Standard Mileage Rates 72
Chapter 10 74
Be's Tax Facts 74
Need a Copy of Your Prior Year Tax Information? 74
AMT… What you should know! 83
Save on Your Taxes and for Retirement with the Saver's Credit 84
Tax Scams for the Filing Season 89
Filing Fake Documents to Hide Income 91

Buzzing Around Tax Facts With Be's

Tax Season Has Started!!!

Greetings from Be's Professional Services, LLC we are your Income Tax Preparation and Bookkeeping Firm.

We service all 50 states!

We offer 4 ways to file with our firm!

They are listed below:

Email: info@besporfessionalservices.com

Fax: 469-454-2575 or

Call your information in 972-296-4237 or 888-707-9915.
(Please be advised that if you call information in we will require you to fax or email your documents within 24 hours for processing.)

File On Line: www.besprofessionalservices.com

Buzzing Around Tax Facts With Be's

Getting to know Be's Professional Services, LLC

We started our journey in January 2010–Present (5 years 10 months). Be's has served many clients regarding their needs in different states. Our company is built with respect, honesty, trust, integrity and loyalty.

Meet the President of Be's Professional Services, LLC

Hi Everyone,

Let me introduce myself, India Roberts is my name and I am the founder and President at Be's Professional Services, LLC.

Be's Professional Services, LLC was started in my home during a time of the unknown. It was a time of truth and understanding. You see Be's is named after my mother who we lost in 2011. Let me share how it all began: It was the best day every when my mother, grandmother and myself was sitting on the couch at my mom's home talking about the old days and how my mother picked cotton for her grandmother.
That Saturday was so exciting and I was getting ready to go back to work on Monday until life happened. That weekend my entire life changed forever. My mom called me and said she wasn't feeling good that night and she needed to go to the hospital.

Buzzing Around Tax Facts With Be's

On the way to the hospital you won't believe what happened. My story is coming soon and I can't wait to share it with you. You can read about the entire journey in my next book which will be out soon. Get ready for Life's Journey. You never know what could happen.

Our Motto: What's important to you is important to us!

Buzzing Around Tax Facts With Be's

Our Services

We serve individual, small corporations, LLC's, partnerships, home-based businesses and sole-proprietorships. We take pride in our ability to make certain that every client receives direction and service based on their individual needs.

Mobile Services Pick up and Drop Off

Individual Tax Services

Federal and State Income Tax Preparation (1040, 1040A, 1040EZ)

Electronic Filing of Tax Returns

Amended Returns

Filing Extensions

IRS Problem Resolution

Tax Education: Personal Consultation & Seminars

We offer Advanced Tax Strategies and Planning: Develop customized strategies that detail the specific steps you need to take to maximize the legal deductions that could possibly save you thousands of dollars in taxes.

Business Tax Services

Business Consulting

Buzzing Around Tax Facts With Be's

Federal and State Income Tax Preparation for:

Sole Proprietorships

S-Corporations

C-Corporations

Partnerships, LLC's, LLP's

Not-for Profit Corporations

IRS Problem Resolution Referral

Buzzing Around Tax Facts With Be's

Contact Be's Professional Services, LLC

Website: www.besprofessionalservices.com

Email: info@besprofessionalservices.com or besprofessionalservices@gmail.com

Like us on Linkedin, Facebook, Instagram, and Twitter

Location: 1536 S. Clark Rd. Duncanville, TX 75137

Phone: (888) 707-9915 or 972-296-4237 4(BES)

Fax: (469) 454-2575

Thanks for your continued support!

Buzzing Around Tax Facts With Be's

Your Bill of Rights as a Taxpayer!

The Taxpayer Bill of Rights is for you to know your rights as a taxpayer!

The Taxpayer Bill of Rights contains 10 provisions.

1. The Right to Be Informed

2. The Right to Quality Service

3. The Right to Pay No More than the Correct Amount of Tax

4. The Right to Challenge the IRS's Position and Be Heard

5. The Right to Appeal an IRS Decision in an Independent Forum

6. The Right to Finality

7. The Right to Privacy

8. The Right to Confidentiality

9. The Right to Retain Representation

10. The Right to a Fair and Just Tax System

2015 Tax Law Updates

Federal Estate Tax Exclusion

The federal estate tax exclusion amount for 2015 is $5,430,000. The exclusion amount for tax year 2014 was $5,340,000.

Federal Gift Tax Exclusion

The federal estate tax exclusion amount for 2015 is $5,430,000. The exclusion amount for tax year 2014 was $5,340,000.

Federal Gift Tax Exclusion

The federal gift tax exclusion for tax year 2015 is $14,000. A taxpayer can exclude $147,000 in gifts given
to a spouse, who is not a citizen of the United States. Gifts exceeding $147,000 must be included in the total amount of taxable gifts for the tax year.

Personal Exemption Amount

The personal exemption amount has been increased for inflation and is $4,000 for 2015. The personal exemption phase-out returned in tax year 2013. Taxpayers whose income exceeds the dollar amount listed in the table below (Beginning Phase-Out) will have their personal exemption(s) reduced by 2% for each increment of $2,500 of their adjusted gross income, which exceeds the applicable amount listed below.

Buzzing Around Tax Facts With Be's

The phase-out for tax year 2015 is shown in the chart below:
Filing Status

	Beginning Phase-out	Completely Phased-out
MFJ/QW	$309,900	$432,400
HH	$284,050	$406,550
Single	$258,250	$380,750
MFS	$154,950	$216,200

Increased Standard Deduction – 2015

Filing Status AND **Standard Deduction**

Single
Under 65 $6,300
65 or older or blind $7,850
65 or older and blind $9,400

Married Filing Jointly
Under 65 (both spouses) $12,600
65 or older or blind (one spouse) $13,850
65 or older or blind (both spouses) $15,100
65 or older and blind (one spouse) $15,100
65 or older and blind (one spouse) and
65 or older or blind (other spouse)
$16,350
65 or older and blind (both spouses) $17,600

Married Filing Separately
Spouse Itemizes Deductions $0
Under 65 $6,300
65 or older or blind $7,550
65 or older and blind $8,800

Buzzing Around Tax Facts With Be's

Head of Household
Under 65 $9,250
65 or older or blind $10,800
65 or older and blind $12,350
Qualifying Widow(er)
Under 65 $12,600
65 or older or blind $13,850
65 or older and blind $15,100

Dependent Standard Deduction

The dependent standard deduction for tax year 2015 is $1,050 for dependents with unearned income only. For dependents who have both earned and unearned income, the standard deduction is the greater of $1,050 or the dependent's earned income plus $350, but not more than the standard deduction for their filing status.

Standard Deduction for Taxpayers Who Are 65 or Older and/or Blind (Born Before January 2, 1951)

Taxpayers who are age 65 or older and/or blind are entitled to an additional standard deduction. This

amount is added to the regular standard deduction based on their filing status. Taxpayers who itemize are not eligible for the additional standard deduction. The additional standard deduction for Married Filing Jointly, Qualifying Widow(er) with Dependent Child and Married Filing Separately individuals is $1,250. Single and Head of Household individuals are allowed an additional standard deduction of $1,550.

Buzzing Around Tax Facts With Be's

2015 Filing Requirements for Most People

Filing requirements are determined by adding the taxpayer's personal exemption and standard deduction together. Therefore is a couple is filing using the Married Filing Jointly status and under age 65, they would have two personal exemptions and a standard deduction of $12,600, for a filing requirement of $20,600.

The filing requirements for tax year 2015 are listed next.

Filing Status AND at the end of 2015 you were

THEN file a return if your

Gross income was at least
Single Under 65 $10,300
65 or older $11,850
Married Filing Jointly Under 65 $20,600
65 or older (1 spouse) $21,850
65 or older (both spouses) $23,100
Married Filing Separately Any age $4,000
Head of Household Under 65 $13,250
65 or older $14,800
Qualifying Widow(er) Under 65 $16,600
65 or older $17,850
If the taxpayer was born on January 1, 1951, he is considered to be age 65 at the end of 2015

Changes to Itemized Deductions

Buzzing Around Tax Facts With Be's

Beginning in 2015, total itemized deductions for taxpayers with adjusted gross income above the following
thresholds may be reduced

- ☐ $309,900 if Married Filing Jointly or Qualifying Widow(er),
- ☐ $284,050 if Head of Household,
- ☐ $258,250 if Single, and
- ☐ $154,950 if Married Filing Separately

Standard Mileage Rates

Business 57.5
Medical/Moving 23
Charitable 14

Earned Income Credit

The maximum amount of the credit for tax year 2015 has increased to $3,359 with one qualifying child, $5,548 for two qualifying children, $6,242 for more than two qualifying children, and $503 with no qualifying
child.

Child Tax Credit

The child tax credit remains at a maximum of $1,000 per qualifying child for tax year 2015.

Earned Income for Additional Child Tax Credit

The earned income threshold generally needed to qualify for the additional child tax credit is $3,000 for tax year 2015.

Adoption Benefits Increased

Buzzing Around Tax Facts With Be's

For 2015 the maximum adoption credit has increased to $13,400.

Education Credit

Taxpayers may deduct up to $2,500 of interest paid on qualified education loans for college or vocational school expenses as an adjustment to income.

American Opportunity and Lifetime Learning Education Credits

The AOC credit is $2,000 or Lifetime Learning Credit is $2,000 per taxpayer, per return.

Maximum Deferrals and Contributions
The maximum regular deferral amount a taxpayer may elect to defer into his 401(k) plan is $18,000 for tax year 2015 ($24,000 for employees age 50 and older). The maximum deferral contribution for SIMPLE plans is $12,500 ($15,500 for employees age 50 and older).

Roth IRA

For 2015, Roth IRA contribution limits are reduced (phased out) based on the following MAGI limitations.
Filing Status Phase-out Begins (Modified AGI) and Phased Out Completely(Modified AGI)

Buzzing Around Tax Facts With Be's

Married Filing Jointly/Qualifying Widow(er) $183,000 /$193,000

Single, Head of Household, Married Filing, Separately and did not live with spouse at any time in 2015 $116,000/ $131,000

Married Filing Separately and lived with spouse at all during 2015 0 $10,000

Foreign Earned Income
The maximum foreign earned income exclusion for tax year 2015 is $100,800 to offset inflation. The maximum amount of foreign housing expenses allowed for 2015 is $30,240 (100,800 X 0.30).

Affordable Care Act (ACA)

The Shared Responsibility Payment is calculated using 2 methods; however, the taxpayer will only pay the higher amount.

1. 2% of the yearly household income for income amounts greater than the filing requirement threshold (see table below) for the taxpayer's filing status or.

2. $325 per person for tax year 2015 ($162.50 per child under age 18),
 limited to a family maximum of $97

Chapter One

What You Need to Know About IRS and Health Care

Information That the Health Coverage Providers Reported to the IRS

For purposes of the health care law, the information that health coverage providers, including employers that provide self-insured coverage, includes the following:

- The name, address, and employer identification number of the provider
- The responsible individual's name, address, and taxpayer identification number – or date of birth if a TIN is not available
- If the responsible individual is not enrolled in the coverage, providers may, but are not required to, report the TIN of the responsible individual
- The name and TIN, or date of birth if a TIN is not available, of each individual covered under the policy or program and the months for which the individual was enrolled in coverage and entitled to receive benefits
- For coverage provided by a health insurance issuer through a group health plan, the name,

Buzzing Around Tax Facts With Be's

address, and EIN of the employer sponsoring the plan, and whether the coverage is a qualified health plan enrolled in through the Small Business Health Options Program – known as SHOP – and the SHOP's identifier

A taxpayer identification number is an identification number used by the IRS in the administration of tax laws. Taxpayer identification numbers include Social Security numbers.

Reporting of TINs for all covered individuals is necessary for the IRS to verify an individual's coverage without the need to contact the individual.

Buzzing Around Tax Facts With Be's

Be's Client Reviews

Danielle Fisher Joyner- *5 star* In fear of owing this year, Be's Professional Service to the rescue. The service was exactly as they say professional. They asked the right questions and maximize my returned. Thank you so very much.

Buzzing Around Tax Facts With Be's

FYI--Affordable Care Act – Individuals

Taxpayers who might qualify for an exemption from having qualifying health coverage and making a payment should call Be's for information about these exemptions. Health Coverage Exemptions are available.

The Affordable Care Act calls for each individual to have qualifying health insurance coverage for each month of the year, have and exemption, or make an individual shared responsibility payment when filing his or her federal income tax return.

You may be exempt if you:

- Have no affordable coverage options because the minimum amount you must pay for the annual premiums is more than eight percent of your household income,
- Have a gap in coverage for less than three consecutive months, or
- Qualify for an exemption for one of several other reasons, including having a hardship that prevents you from obtaining coverage or belonging to a group explicitly exempt from the requirement.

How you get an exemption depends upon the type of exemption. You can obtain some exemptions only from the Market Place in the area where you live, others only from the IRS when you file your income tax return, and others from either the Marketplace or the IRS.

Buzzing Around Tax Facts With Be's

The Individual Shared Responsibility Provision

The individual responsibility requires that you and each member of your family have qualifying health insurance, a health coverage exemption, or make a payment when you file your taxes.

Who is subject to the individual shared responsibility provision?

The provision applies to individuals of all ages, including children. The adult or married couple who can claim a child or another individual as a dependent for federal income tax purposes is responsible for making the payment if the dependent does not have coverage or an exemption.

When does the individual shared responsibility provision go into effect?

The provision went into effect on Jan. 1, 2014. It applies to each month in the calendar year

What happens if I owe an individual shared responsibility payment, but I cannot afford to make the payment when filing my tax return?

The IRS routinely works with taxpayers who owe amounts they cannot afford to pay.

Chapter Two

Employers and the IRS

ACA Information for Employers Counting Full-time and Full-time Equivalent Employees

The Affordable Care Act: Employers average their number of employees across the months in the year to see whether they will be an applicable large employer.

To determine if your organization is an applicable large employer for a year, count your organization's full-time employees and full-time equivalent employees for each month of the prior year.

If you are a member of an aggregated group, count the full-time employees and full-time equivalent employees of all members of the group for each month of the prior year. Then average the numbers for the year.

Employers with 50 or more full-time equivalent employees are applicable large employers and will need to file an annual information return reporting whether and what health insurance they offered

Buzzing Around Tax Facts With Be's

employees. In addition, they are subject to the Employer Shared Responsibility requirement.

FYI:

- **A full-time employee** is an employee who is employed on average, per month, at least 30 hours of service per week, or at least 130 hours of service in a calendar month.
- **A full-time equivalent employee** is a combination of employees, each of whom individually is not a full-time employee, but who, in combination, are equivalent to a full-time employee.
- **An aggregated group** is commonly owned or otherwise related or affiliated employers, which must combine their employees to determine their workforce size.

A.C.A. and Employers Understanding Affordable and Minimum Value Coverage

FYI: Under the employer shared responsibility provisions of the Affordable Care Act, large employers may either offer affordable minimum essential coverage that provides minimum value to its full-time employees and their dependents or potentially owe an employer shared responsibility payment to the IRS.

Here are definitions to help you understand affordable coverage and minimum value coverage.

Affordable coverage: If the lowest cost self-only only health plan is 9.5 percent or less of your full-time employee's household income then the coverage is considered affordable. Because you likely will not know your employee's household income, for purposes of the employer shared responsibility provisions, you can determine whether you offered affordable coverage under various safe harbors based on information available to the employer.

Minimum value coverage: An employer-sponsored plan provides minimum value if it covers at least 60 percent of the total allowed cost of benefits that are expected to be incurred under the plan.

Under existing guidance, employers generally must use a minimum value calculator developed by HHS to determine if a plan with standard features provides minimum value. Plans with nonstandard features are required to obtain an actuarial certification for the nonstandard features. The guidance also describes

Buzzing Around Tax Facts With Be's

certain safe harbor plan designs that will satisfy minimum value.

If you have questions call Be's Professional Services

Buzzing Around Tax Facts With Be's

Be's Client Reviews

I highly recommend the services of Be's Professional Services. Oh they have a kid's zone for children to play while parents tend to their taxes.

Chapter Three

How Getting Married/ Divorced Can Affect Your Taxes

Getting Married Can Affect Your Premium Tax Credit

Did you know that the Marketplace can be opened if you have a life changing event?

If you, your spouse or a dependent gets health insurance coverage through the Marketplace, you need to let the Marketplace know you got married. Informing the Marketplace about changes in circumstances, such as marriage or divorce, allows the Marketplace to help make sure you have the right coverage for you and your family and adjust the amount of advance credit payments that the government sends to your health insurer.

Reporting the changes will help you avoid having too much or not enough premium assistance paid to reduce your monthly health insurance premiums. Getting too much premium assistance means you may owe additional money or get a smaller refund when you file your taxes. Getting too little could mean missing out on monthly premium assistance that you deserve. You should also check whether getting

Buzzing Around Tax Facts With Be's

married affects your, your spouse's, or your dependents' eligibility for coverage through your employer or your spouse's employer, because that will affect your eligibility for the premium tax credit.

Other changes in circumstances that you should report to the Marketplace include:

- the birth or adoption of a child,
- divorce,
- getting or losing a job,
- moving to a new address, gaining or losing eligibility for employer or government sponsored health care coverage, and
- any other changes that might affect family composition, family size, income or your enrollment.

Key Tax Tips for Divorce or Separation

Income tax may be the last thing on your mind after a divorce or separation. However, these events can have a big impact on your taxes. Alimony and a name change are just a few items you may need to consider.

Key tax tips to keep in mind if you get divorced or separated.

- **Child Support.** If you pay child support, you can't deduct it on your tax return. If you receive child support, the amount you receive is not taxable.
- **Alimony Paid.** If you make payments under a divorce or separate maintenance decree or written separation agreement you may be able to deduct them as alimony. This applies only if the payments qualify as alimony for federal tax purposes. If the decree or agreement does not require the payments, they do not qualify as alimony.
- **Alimony Received.** If you get alimony from your spouse or former spouse, it is taxable in the year you get it. Alimony is not subject to tax withholding so you may need to increase the tax you pay during the year to avoid a penalty.
- **Spousal IRA.** If you get a final decree of divorce or separate maintenance by the end of your tax year, you can't deduct contributions you make to your former spouse's traditional IRA. You may be able to deduct contributions you make to your own traditional IRA.

Buzzing Around Tax Facts With Be's

- **Name Changes.** If you change your name after your divorce, notify the Social Security Administration of the change. A name mismatch can delay your refund.

Health Care Law Considerations

- **Special Marketplace Enrollment Period.** If you lose your health insurance coverage due to divorce, you are still required to have coverage for every month of the year for yourself and the dependents you can claim on your tax return. Losing coverage through a divorce is considered a qualifying life event that allows you to enroll in health coverage through the Health Insurance Marketplace.
- **Changes in Circumstances.** If you purchase health insurance coverage through the Health Insurance Marketplace, you may get advance payments of the premium tax credit in 2015. If you do, you should report changes in circumstances to your Marketplace throughout the year. Changes to report include a change in marital
-
- status, a name change and a change in your income or family size. By reporting changes, you will help make sure that you get the proper type and amount of financial assistance. This will also help you avoid getting too much or too little credit in advance.
- **Shared Policy Allocation.** If you divorced or are legally separated during the tax year and are enrolled in the same qualified health plan, you and your former spouse must allocate policy amounts on your separate tax returns to figure

36

Buzzing Around Tax Facts With Be's

your premium tax credit and reconcile any advance payments made on your behalf.

Buzzing Around Tax Facts With Be's

Be's Client Reviews

Lakesha Puryear- Figurer- _5 star_ Very professional company that really cares about you

Chapter Four

How to Get Tax Credits For Childcare and Education

Get Credit for Child and Dependent Care This Summer

Many parents pay for childcare or day camps in the summer while they work. If this applies to you, your costs may qualify for a federal tax credit that can lower your taxes. Here are 10 facts that you should know about the Child and Dependent Care Credit:

1. Your expenses must be for the care of one or more qualifying persons. Your dependent child or children under age 13 usually qualify.

2. Your expenses for care must be work-related. This means that you must pay for the care so you can work or look for work. This rule also applies to your spouse if you file a joint return. Your spouse meets this rule during any month they are a full-time student. They also meet it if they're physically or mentally incapable of self-care.

Buzzing Around Tax Facts With Be's

3. You must have earned income, such as from wages, salaries and tips. It also includes net earnings from self-employment. Your spouse must also have earned income if you file jointly. Your spouse is treated as having earned income for any month that they are a full-time student or incapable of self-care. This rule also applies to you if you file a joint return.

4. As a rule, if you're married you must file a joint return to take the credit. But this rule doesn't apply if you're legally separated or if you and your spouse live apart.

5. You may qualify for the credit whether you pay for care at home, at a daycare facility or at a day camp.

6. The credit is a percentage of the qualified expenses you pay. It can be as much as 35 percent of your expenses, depending on your income.

7. The total expense that you can use for the credit in a year is limited. The limit is $3,000 for one qualifying person or $6,000 for two or more.

8. Overnight camp or summer school tutoring costs do not qualify. You can't include the cost of care provided by your spouse or your child who is under age 19 at the end of the year. You also cannot count the cost of care given by a person you can claim as your dependent. Special rules apply if you get dependent care benefits from your employer.

9. Keep all your receipts and records. Make sure to note the name, address and Social Security number or

Buzzing Around Tax Facts With Be's

employer identification number of the care provider. You must report this information when you claim the credit on your tax return.

10. Remember that this credit is not just a summer tax benefit. You may be able to claim it for care you pay for throughout the year.

Education Tax Credits

Did you pay for college in 2014? If you did it can mean tax savings on your federal tax return.

There are two education credits that can help you with the cost of higher education.

The credits may reduce the amount of tax you owe on your tax return. Here are some important facts you should know about education tax credits.

American Opportunity Tax Credit:

- You may be able to claim up to $2,500 per eligible student.
- The credit applies to the first four years at an eligible college or vocational school.
- It reduces the amount of tax you owe. If the credit reduces your tax to less than zero, you may receive up to $1,000 as a refund.
- It is available for students earning a degree or other recognized credential.

Buzzing Around Tax Facts With Be's

Lifetime Learning Credit:

- The credit is limited to $2,000 per tax return, per year.
- The credit applies to all years of higher education. This includes classes for learning or improving job skills.
- The credit is limited to the amount of your taxes.
- Costs that apply to the credit include the cost of tuition, required fees, books, supplies and equipment that you must buy from the school.

Chapter Five

Moving or Selling Your Home and the IRS

Moving Can Affect Your Premium Tax Credit

If you moved recently, you've probably notified the U.S. Postal Service, utility companies, financial institutions and employers of your new address. If you get health insurance coverage through a Health Insurance Marketplace, the IRS reminds you about one more important notification to add to your list – the Marketplace.

If you are receiving advance payments of the premium tax credit, it is particularly important that you report changes in circumstances, including moving, to the Marketplace. There's a simple reason. Reporting your move lets the Marketplace update the information used to determine your eligibility for a Marketplace plan, which may affect the appropriate amount of advance payments of the premium tax credit that the government sends to your health insurer on your behalf.

Buzzing Around Tax Facts With Be's

Reporting the changes will help you avoid having too much or not enough premium assistance paid to reduce your monthly health insurance premiums. Getting too much premium assistance means you may owe additional money or get a smaller refund when you file your taxes. On the other hand, getting too little could mean missing out on monthly premium assistance that you deserve.

Changes in circumstances that you should report to the Marketplace include, but are not limited to:

- an increase or decrease in your income
- marriage or divorce
- the birth or adoption of a child
- starting a job with health insurance
- gaining or losing your eligibility for other health care coverage

Many of these changes in circumstances – including moving out of the area served by your current Marketplace plan – qualify you for a special enrollment period to change or get insurance through the Marketplace. In most cases, if you qualify for the special enrollment period, you will have sixty days to enroll following the change in circumstances. You can find information about special enrollment periods at healthcare.gov.

Buzzing Around Tax Facts With Be's

Here Are Ten Tax Facts To Know If You Sell Your Home!!

Do you know that if you sell your home and make a profit, the gain may not be taxable? That's just one key tax rule that you should know. Here are ten facts to keep in mind if you sell your home this year.

1. If you have a capital gain on the sale of your home, you may be able to exclude your gain from tax. This rule may apply if you owned and used it as your main home for at least two out of the five years before the date of sale.

2. There are exceptions to the ownership and use rules. Some exceptions apply to persons with a disability. Some apply to certain members of the military and certain government and Peace Corps workers.

3. The most gain you can exclude is $250,000. This limit is $500,000 for joint returns. The net investment tax will not apply to the excluded gain.

4. If the gain is not taxable, you may not need to report the sale to the IRS on your tax return.

5. You must report the sale on your tax return if you can't exclude all or part of the gain. And you must report the sale if you choose not to claim the exclusion. That's also true if you get Form 1099-S, Proceeds from Real Estate Transactions.

Buzzing Around Tax Facts With Be's

6. Generally, you can exclude the gain from the sale of your main home only once every two years.

7. If you own more than one home, you may only exclude the gain on the sale of your main home. Your main home usually is the home that you live in most of the time.

8. If you claimed the first-time homebuyer credit when you bought the home, special rules apply to the sale.

9. If you sell your main home at a loss, you can't deduct it.

10. After you sell your home and move, be sure to give your new address to the IRS.

Buzzing Around Tax Facts With Be's

Be's Client Reviews

Lisa Dunn Robinson- *5 star* A very professional and caring business that caters to your needs

Chapter Six

Tips/Facts You Should Know When Filling an Amended Return

Tax Tips about Filing an Amended Tax Return

When to amend. You should amend your tax return if you need to correct your filing status, the number of dependents you claimed, or your total income. You should also amend your return to claim tax deductions or tax credits that you did not claim when you filed your original return.

Amending to claim an additional refund. If you are waiting for a refund from your original tax return, don't file your amended return until after you receive the refund. You may cash the refund check from your original return. Amended returns take up to 16 weeks to process.

Buzzing Around Tax Facts With Be's

Amending to pay additional tax. If you're filing amended tax returns because you owe more tax let us amend your return for you. You will have to pay the tax as soon as possible. This will limit interest and penalty charges.

Health Care Forms. If you or anyone on your return enrolled in qualifying health care coverage through the Health Insurance Marketplace, you should have received a form called the Health Insurance Marketplace Statement.

You may also want to file an amended return if:

- You filed and incorrectly claimed a premium tax credit, or
- You filed an income tax return and failed to file for the Premium Tax Credit, to reconcile your advance payments of the premium tax credit.

Track your return. You can track the status of your amended tax return three weeks after you file.

Buzzing Around Tax Facts With Be's

Nine Facts on Filing an Amended Return

An amended tax return generally allows you to file again to correct your filing status, your income or to add deductions or credits you may have missed.

Here are nine points the IRS wants you to know about amending your federal income tax return.

1. Use Form 1040X, Amended U.S. Individual Income Tax Return, to file an amended income tax return.

2.

3. Use Form 1040X to correct previously filed Forms 1040, 1040A or 1040EZ. An amended return cannot be filed electronically, thus you must file it by paper.

4. Generally, you do not need to file an amended return due to math errors. The IRS will automatically make that correction. Also, do not file an amended return because you forgot to attach tax forms such as W-2s or schedules. The IRS normally will send a request asking for those.

5. Be sure to enter the year of the return you are amending at the top of Form 1040X. Generally, you must file Form 1040X within three years

Buzzing Around Tax Facts With Be's

from the date you filed your original return or within two years from the date you paid the tax, whichever is later.

6. If you are amending more than one tax return, prepare a 1040X for each return and mail them in separate envelopes to the appropriate IRS campus. The 1040X instructions list the addresses for the campuses.

7. If the changes involve another schedule or form, you must attach that schedule or form to the amended return.

8. If you are filing to claim an additional refund, wait until you have received your original refund before filing Form 1040X. You may cash that check while waiting for any additional refund.

9. If you owe additional 2010 tax, file Form 1040X and pay the tax before the due date to limit interest and penalty charges that could accrue on your account. Interest is charged on any tax not paid by the due date of the original return, without regard to extensions.

Chapter Seven

Tips You Should Know When Giving To Charity

501(c) (3) Exemption Requirements

To be tax-exempt under section 501(c)(3) of the Internal Revenue Code, an organization must be organized and operated exclusively for exempt organization set forth in section 501(c)(3), and none of its earnings may inure to any private shareholder or individual. In addition, it may not be an action organization, *i.e.,* it may not attempt to influence legislation as a substantial part of its activities and it may not participate in any campaign activity for or against political candidates.

Organizations described in section 501(c) (3) are commonly referred to as *charitable organizations*. Organizations described in section 501(c) (3), other than testing for public safety organizations, are eligible to receive tax-deductible contributions in accordance with Code.

Buzzing Around Tax Facts With Be's

The organization must not be organized or operated for the benefit of private interests, and no part of a section 501(c)(3) organization's net earnings may inure to the benefit of any private shareholder or individual. If the organization engages in an excess benefit transaction with a person having substantial influence over the organization, an excise tax may be imposed on the person and any organization managers agreeing to the transaction.

Section 501(c) (3) organizations are restricted in how much political and legislative (*lobbying*) activities they may conduct.

Buzzing Around Tax Facts With Be's

Visit our Facebook page
https://www.facebook.com/taxseasonready

Be's Professional Services
INCOME TAX
Copying & Printing · Notary Public · Tax Preparation

Buzzing Around Tax Facts With Be's

Tips for Year-End Gifts to Charity

Many people give to charity each year during the holiday season. Remember, if you want to claim a tax deduction for your gifts, you must itemize your deductions. There are several tax rules that you should know about before you give. Here are six tips from the IRS that you should keep in mind:

1. Qualified charities. You can only deduct gifts you give to qualified charities. Remember that you can deduct donations you give to churches, synagogues, temples, mosques and government agencies.

2. Monetary donations. Gifts of money include those made in cash or by check, electronic funds transfer, credit card and payroll deduction. You must have a bank record or a written statement from the charity to deduct any gift of money on your tax return. This is true regardless of the amount of the gift. The statement must show the name of the charity and the date and amount of the contribution. Bank records include canceled checks, or bank, credit union and credit card statements. If you give by payroll deductions, you should retain a pay stub, a Form W-2 wage statement or other document from your employer. It must show the total amount withheld for charity, along with the pledge card showing the name of the charity.

3. Household goods. Household items include furniture, furnishings, electronics, appliances and linens. If you donate clothing and household items to charity they generally must be in at least good used condition to claim a tax deduction. If you claim a deduction of over $500 for an item it doesn't have to

56

Buzzing Around Tax Facts With Be's

meet this standard if you include a qualified appraisal of the item with your tax return.

4. Records required. You must get an acknowledgment from the charity for each deductible Donation (either money or property) of $250 or more. Additional rules apply to the statement for gifts of that amount. This statement is in addition to the records required for deducting cash gifts. However, one statement with all of the required information may meet both requirements.

5. Year-end gifts. You can deduct contributions in the year you make them. If you charge your gift to a credit card before the end of the year it will count for 2015. This is true even if you don't pay the credit card bill until 2015. Also, a check will count for 2015 as long as you mail it in 2015.

Buzzing Around Tax Facts With Be's

Tips on Travel While Giving Your Services to Charity

Do you plan to donate your services to charity this summer? Will you travel as part of the service?

If so, some travel expenses may help lower your taxes when you file your tax return next year.

Here are some tax tips that you should know if you travel while giving your services to charity.

Qualified Charities. In order to deduct your costs, your volunteer work must be for a qualified charity. Most groups must apply to the IRS to become qualified. Churches and governments are qualified, and do not need to apply to the IRS.

Out-of-Pocket Expenses. You may be able to deduct some costs you pay to give your services. This can include the cost of travel. The costs must be necessary while you are away from home giving your services for a qualified charity. All costs must be:

Buzzing Around Tax Facts With Be's

o Unreimbursed,

o Directly connected with the services,

o Expenses you had only because of the services you gave, and

o Not personal, living or family expenses

- **Genuine and Substantial Duty.** Your charity work has to be real and substantial throughout the trip. You can't deduct expenses if you only have nominal duties or do not have any duties for significant parts of the trip.
-
- **Value of Time or Service.** You can't deduct the value of your services that you give to charity. This includes income lost while you work as an unpaid volunteer for a qualified charity.
-
- **Deductible travel.** The types of expenses that you may be able to deduct include:

Air, rail and bus transportation,

Car expenses,

Lodging costs,

The cost of meals

Buzzing Around Tax Facts With Be's

IRS.... Tax Guidance Related to Ebola Outbreak in Guinea, Liberia and Sierra Leone

The Internal Revenue Service today issued two items of guidance in response to the need for charitable and other relief due to the Ebola outbreak in Guinea, Liberia and Sierra Leone. One provides special relief intended to support leave-based donation programs to aid victims who have suffered from the Ebola outbreak in those countries. The other designates the Ebola outbreak in those countries as a qualified disaster for federal tax purposes.

Under the leave base donation guidance, employees may donate their vacation, sick or personal leave in exchange for employer cash payments made to qualified tax-exempt organizations providing relief for the victims of the Ebola outbreak in Guinea, Liberia or Sierra Leone. Employees can forgo leave in exchange for employer cash payments made before Jan. 1, 2016. Under this special relief, the donated leave will not be included in the income or wages of the employees. Employers will be permitted to deduct the amount of the cash payment.

For example, if an American company has such a program and makes a cash donation of the value of an employee's donated leave before January 1, 2016, to

Buzzing Around Tax Facts With Be's

an organization that is providing medical services and supplies for the relief of victims of the Ebola outbreak in Guinea, Liberia, or Sierra Leone, the IRS will not consider the amount of that payment as gross income or wages of the employee. Additionally, the IRS will not assert that the U.S. Company can only deduct such cash payments under Internal Revenue Code section 170.

Chapter Eight

Tax Breaks and Benefits for Military

Tax Benefits for Members of the Armed Forces

Special tax benefits apply to members of the U. S. Armed Forces. For example, some types of pay are not taxable. And special rules may apply to some tax deductions, credits and deadlines. Here are some of those benefits:

1. **Deadline Extensions.** Some members of the military, such as those who serve in a combat zone, can postpone some tax deadlines if this applies to you, you can get automatic extensions of time to file your tax return and to pay your taxes.
2. **Combat Pay Exclusion.** If you serve in a combat zone, certain combat pay is not taxable. You won't need to show the pay on your tax return because combat pay isn't included in the wages reported on your Form W-2, Wage and Tax Statement. Service in support of a combat zone may qualify for this exclusion.

Buzzing Around Tax Facts With Be's

3. **Earned Income Tax Credit.** If you get nontaxable combat pay, you may choose to include it to come up with EITC. You would make this choice if it increases your credit. Even if you do, the combat pay stays nontaxable.
4. **Moving Expense Deduction.** You may be able to deduct some of your unreimbursed moving costs. This applies if the move is due to a permanent change of station.
5. **Uniform Deduction.** You can deduct the costs of certain uniforms that regulations prohibit you from wearing while off duty. This includes the costs of purchase and upkeep. You must reduce your deduction by any allowance you get for these costs.
6. **Signing Joint Returns.** Both spouses normally must sign a joint income tax return. If your spouse is absent due to certain military duty or conditions, you may be able to sign for your spouse. In other cases
7. when your spouse is absent, you may need a power of attorney to file a joint return.
8. **Reservists' Travel Deduction.** If you're a member of the U.S. Armed Forces Reserves, you may deduct certain costs of travel on your tax return. This applies to the unreimbursed costs of travel to perform your reserve duties that are more than 100 miles away from home.
9. **Nontaxable ROTC Allowances.** Active duty ROTC pay, such as pay for summer advanced camp, is taxable. But some amounts paid to ROTC students in advanced training are not taxable. This applies to educational and subsistence allowances.
10. **Civilian Life.** If you leave the military and look for work, you may be able to deduct some

Buzzing Around Tax Facts With Be's

job hunting expenses. You may be able to include the costs of travel, preparing a resume and job placement agency fees. Moving expenses may also qualify for a tax deduction.

Buzzing Around Tax Facts With Be's

Tips about Tax Breaks for the Military

If you are in the U. S. Armed Forces, special tax breaks may apply to you. For example, some types of pay are not taxable.

Certain rules apply to deductions or credits that you may be able to claim that can lower your tax. In some cases, you may get more time to file your tax return.

Deadline Extensions. Some members of the military, such as those who serve in a combat zone, can postpone some tax deadlines. If this applies to you, you can get automatic extension of time to file your tax return and to pay your taxes.

Combat Pay Exclusion. If you serve in a combat zone, certain combat pay you get is not taxable. You won't need to show the pay on your tax return because combat pay is not part of the wages reported on your Form W-2, Wage and Tax Statement. If you serve in support of a combat zone, you may qualify for this exclusion.

Earned Income Tax Credit or EITC. If you get nontaxable combat pay, you can include it to find out

65

Buzzing Around Tax Facts With Be's

EITC. Doing so may boost your credit. Even if you do, the combat pay stays nontaxable.

Moving Expense Deduction. You may be able to deduct some of your unreimbursed moving costs. This applies if the move is due to a permanent change of station.

Uniform Deduction. You can deduct the costs of certain uniforms that you can't wear while off duty. This includes the costs of purchase and upkeep. You must reduce your deduction by any allowance you get for these costs.

Signing Joint Returns. Both spouses normally must sign a joint income tax return. If your spouse is absent due to certain military duty or conditions, you may be able to sign for your spouse. In other cases when your spouse is absent, you may need a power of attorney to file a joint return.

Reservists' Travel Deduction. If you're a member of the U.S. Armed Forces Reserves, you may deduct certain costs of travel on your tax return. This applies

Buzzing Around Tax Facts With Be's

to the unreimbursed costs of travel to perform your reserve duties that are more than 100 miles away from home.

ROTC Allowances. Some amounts paid to ROTC students in advanced training are not taxable. This applies to allowances for education and subsistence. Active duty ROTC pay is taxable. For instance, pay for summer advanced camp is taxable.

Civilian Life. If you leave the military and look for work, you may be able to deduct some job search expenses. You may be able to include the costs of travel, preparing a resume and job placement agency fees. Moving expenses may also qualify for a tax deduction.

Please be advised that it is always exceptions to the rules.

Chapter Nine

Running Your Own Business to Looking For a Job Tax Tips

Five Basic Tax Tips for New Businesses

If you start a business, one key to success is to know about your federal tax obligations. You may need to know not only about income taxes but also about payroll taxes. Here are five basic tax tips that can help get your business off to a good start.

1. Business Structure. As you start out, you'll need to choose the business structure. Some common types include sole proprietorship, partnership and corporation. You may also choose to be an S corporation or Limited Liability Company. You'll report your business activity using the IRS forms which are right for your business type.

2. Business Taxes. There are four general types of business tax. They are income tax, self-employment tax, employment tax and excise tax. The type of taxes your business pays usually depends on which type of business you choose to set up. You may need to pay your taxes by making estimated tax payments.

Buzzing Around Tax Facts With Be's

3. Employer Identification Number. You may have to get an EIN for federal tax purposes.

4. Accounting Method. An accounting method is a set of rules that determine when to report income and expenses. Your business must use a consistent method. The two that are most common are the cash method and the accrual method. Under the cash method, you normally report income in the year that you receive it and deduct expenses in the year that you pay them. Under the accrual method, you generally report income in the year that you earn it and deduct expenses in the year that you incur them. This is true even if you receive the income or pay the expenses in a future year.

5. Employee Health Care. The (SBHCTC) Small Business Health Care Tax Credit helps small businesses and tax-exempt organizations pay for health care coverage they offer their employees. A small employer is eligible for the credit if it has fewer than 25 employees who work full-time, or a combination of full-time and part-time. Beginning in 2014, the maximum credit is 50 percent of premiums paid for small business employers and 35 percent of premiums paid for small tax-exempt employers, such as charities.

For 2015 and after, employers employing at least a certain number of employees (generally 50 full-time employees or a combination of full-time and part-time employees that is equivalent to 50 full-time

Buzzing Around Tax Facts With Be's

employees) will be subject to the employer shared responsibility act.

Buzzing Around Tax Facts With Be's

Job Hunting Expenses

Many people change their job in the summer. If you look for a new job in the same line of work, you may be able to deduct some of your job hunting costs.

Here are some key tax facts you should know about if you search for a new job:

- **Same Occupation.** Your expenses must be for a job search in your current line of work. You can't deduct expenses for a job search in a new occupation.
- **Résumé Costs.** You can deduct the cost of preparing and mailing your résumé.
- **Travel Expenses.** If you travel to look for a new job, you may be able to deduct the cost of the trip. To deduct the cost of the travel to and from the area, the trip must be mainly to look for a new job. You may still be able to deduct some costs if looking for a job is not the main purpose of the trip.
- **Placement Agency.** You can deduct some job placement agency fees you pay to look for a job.
- **First Job.** You can't deduct job search expenses if you're looking for a job for the first time.
- **Work-Search Break.** You can't deduct job search expenses if there was a long break between the end of your last job and the time you began looking for a new one.
- **Reimbursed Costs.** Reimbursed expenses are not deductible.

Buzzing Around Tax Facts With Be's

- **Schedule A.** You usually deduct your job search expenses on Schedule A, Itemized Deductions. You'll claim them as a miscellaneous deduction. You can deduct the total miscellaneous deductions that are more than two percent of your adjusted gross income.
- **Premium Tax Credit.** If you receive advance payment of the premium credit card in 2014 it is important that you report changes in circumstances, such as changes in your income or family size, to your Health Insurance Marketplace. Advance payments of the premium tax credit provide financial assistance to help you pay for the insurance you buy through the Health Insurance Marketplace. Reporting changes will help you get the proper type and amount of financial assistance so you can avoid getting too much or too little in advance.

How to Book Returned or Postdated Checks

To avoid mispostings—and liability for another employee's misdeeds—follow these simple steps:

Returned checks. When the bank notifies you that it is returning a customer's check for NSF (not sufficient funds), debit the customer's account immediately—even if you plan to redeposit the check the same day. For good internal controls, instruct your bank to address all returned checks to someone other than you—possibly the owner or a senior manager. This can protect you if an employee tries to use fictitious checks to cover temporary shortages.

Postdated checks. If a customer gives you postdated checks, treat them as a *Note Receivable*. In other words, debit it to Notes Receivable, not to Cash. On the date written on the check, deposit it to your firm's account, debiting Cash and crediting Notes Receivable

Buzzing Around Tax Facts With Be's

New Standard Mileage Rates

The Internal Revenue Service today issued the 2015 optional standard mileage rates used to calculate the deductible costs of operating an automobile for business, charitable, medical or moving purposes.

Beginning on Jan. 1, 2015, the standard mileage rates for the use of a car, van, pickup or panel truck will be:

- 57.5 cents per mile for business miles driven, up from 56 cents in 2014
- 23 cents per mile driven for medical or moving purposes, down half a cent from 2014
- 14 cents per mile driven in service of charitable organizations

The standard mileage rate for business is based on an annual study of the fixed and variable costs of operating an automobile, including depreciation, insurance, repairs, tires, maintenance, gas and oil. The rate for medical and moving purposes is based on the variable costs, such as gas and oil. The charitable rate is set by law.

Buzzing Around Tax Facts With Be's

Taxpayers always have the option of claiming deductions based on the actual costs of using a vehicle rather than the standard mileage rates.

Chapter 10

Be's Tax Facts

Need a Copy of Your Prior Year Tax Information?

There are many reasons you may need a copy of your tax return information from a prior year. You may need it when applying for a student loan, home mortgage or for a VISA. If you don't have your copy, Be's Professional Services can help you get your tax information.

There are 2 types of return information we can get for you.

Tax Return Transcript. A return transcript shows most line items from your tax return just as you filed it.

Buzzing Around Tax Facts With Be's

Tax Account Transcript. This transcript shows any adjustments made by you or the IRS after you filed your return.

Be's Professional Services can assist you in obtaining any documents from the IRS please allow 5 to 10 days.

Buzzing Around Tax Facts With Be's

Get Prior Year Tax Information

- **Tax Return Transcript.** This shows most line items from your tax return as originally filed, along with any forms and schedules from your return. This transcript does not reflect any changes made to the return after you filed it. Tax return transcripts are free. After the IRS has processed a return, transcripts are available for the current tax year and the past three tax years. This is the information that is very important.

- **Order a Transcript.** You can request both transcript types online, by phone or by mail.

- **Tax Return Copies.** Actual copies of your tax returns are generally available for the current tax year and as far back as six years. The fee for each copy you order will vary.

-

IRS Offers Tips for Taxpayers Who Missed the Tax Deadline

Buzzing Around Tax Facts With Be's

- **File as soon as possible.** If you owe federal income tax, you should file and pay as soon as you can to minimize any penalty and interest charges. There is no penalty for filing a late return if you are due a refund.

- **Penalties and interest may be due.** If you missed the April 15 deadline, you may have to pay penalties and interest. The IRS may charge penalties for late filing and for late payment. The law generally does not allow a waiver of interest charges. However, the IRS will

-

- consider a reduction of these penalties if you can show a reasonable cause for being late.

- **E-file is your best option.** IRS e-file programs are available through Oct. 15. E-file is the easiest, safest and most accurate way to file. With e-file, you will receive confirmation that the IRS has received your tax return. If you e-file and are due a refund, the IRS will normally issue it within 21 days.

- **Pay as much as you can.** If you owe tax but can't pay it all at once, you should pay as much as you can when you file your tax return. Pay

Buzzing Around Tax Facts With Be's

the remaining balance due as soon as possible to minimize penalties and interest charges.

- **Installment Agreements are available.** If you need more time to pay your federal income taxes, you can request a payment agreement with the IRS.

- **Refunds may be waiting.** If you're due a refund, you should file as soon as possible to get it. Even if you are not required to file, you may be entitled to a refund.

Last-Minute Filers: Avoiding Some Common Errors

Here are some ways to avoid common mistakes.

File electronically. Filing electronically or e-file vastly reduces tax return errors, as the tax software does the calculations, flags common errors and prompts taxpayers for missing information.

Mail a paper return to the right address.

Take a close look at the tax tables. When figuring tax using the tax table, taxpayers should be sure to use the correct column for the filing status claimed.

Fill in all requested information clearly. When entering information on the tax return, including Social Security numbers, take the time to be sure it is correct and easy to read. Also, check only one filing status and the appropriate exemption boxes.

Buzzing Around Tax Facts With Be's

Review all figures. While software catches and prevents many errors on e-file returns, math errors remain common on paper returns.

Get the right routing and account numbers.

Sign and date the return.

Attach all required forms. Paper filers need to attach W-2s and other forms that reflect tax withholding, to the front of their returns.

Keep a copy of the return.

Request a Filing Extension. For taxpayers who cannot meet the April 15 deadline, requesting a filing extension is easy and will prevent late filing penalties.

But keep in mind that while an extension grants additional time to file, tax payments are still due April 15.

Buzzing Around Tax Facts With Be's

Owe tax? Get on a Payment Plan...Send What You Can!!!

Buzzing Around Tax Facts With Be's

Reduce Your Taxes with Miscellaneous Deductions

If you itemize deductions on your tax return, you may be able to deduct certain miscellaneous expenses. You may benefit from this because a tax deduction normally reduces your federal income tax.

Here are some things you should know about miscellaneous deductions:

Deductions Subject to the Two Percent Limit.

You can deduct most miscellaneous expenses only if they exceed two percent of your adjusted gross income. These include expenses such as:

- Unreimbursed employee expenses.
- Expenses related to searching for a new job in the same profession.
- Certain work clothes and uniforms.
- Tools needed for your job.
- Union dues.
- Work-related travel and transportation.

Make sure you are aware of all the will benefit you and our family.

AMT... What you should know!

Even if you've never paid the Alternative Minimum Tax, before, you should not ignore this tax. Your taxes may have changed so that this may be the year that you need to pay AMT.

You may have to pay this tax if your income is above a certain amount.

AMT attempts to ensure that taxpayers who claim certain tax benefits pay a minimum amount of tax.

Here is something that you should know about the AMT:

When AMT applies. You may have to pay the AMT if your taxable income, plus certain adjustments, is more than your exemption amount. Your filing status and income determine the amount of your exemption.

Save on Your Taxes and for Retirement with the Saver's Credit

If you contribute to a retirement plan, like a 401(k) or an IRA, you may be able to claim the Saver's Credit. This credit can help you save for retirement and reduce the tax you owe. Here are some key facts that you should know about this important tax credit:

Formal Name. The formal name of the Saver's Credit is the Retirement Savings Contribution Credit. The Saver's Credit is in addition to other tax savings you get if you set aside money for retirement. For example, you may be able to deduct your contributions to a traditional IRA.

• **Maximum Credit.** The Saver's Credit is worth up to $2,000 if you are married and file a joint return. The credit is worth up to $1,000 if you are single. The credit you receive is often much less than the maximum. This is due in part because of the deductions and other credits you may claim.

• **Income Limits.** You may be able to claim the credit depending on your filing status and the amount of your yearly income.

Buzzing Around Tax Facts With Be's

You may be eligible for the credit on your 2014 tax return if you are:

Married filing jointly with income up to $60,000

Head of household with income up to $45,000

Married filing separately or a single taxpayer with income up to $30,000

• **Other Rules.** Other rules that apply to the credit include:

You must be at least 18 years of age.

You can't have been a full-time student in 2015.

No other person can claim you as a dependent on their tax return.

Buzzing Around Tax Facts With Be's

Things to Know about Identity Theft and Your Taxes

Learning you are a victim of identity theft can be a stressful event. Identity theft is also a challenge to businesses, organizations and government agencies, including the IRS. Tax-related identity theft occurs when someone uses your stolen Social Security number to file a tax return claiming a fraudulent refund.

Many times, you may not be aware that someone has stolen your identity. The IRS may be the first to let you know you're a victim of ID theft after you try to file your taxes.

Here are some things to know about ID Theft:

Protect your Records. Do not carry your Social Security card or other documents with your SSN on them.

Don't Fall for Scams. The IRS will not call you to demand immediate payment, nor will it call about

Buzzing Around Tax Facts With Be's

taxes owed without first mailing you a bill. Be aware of threatening phone calls from someone claiming to be from the IRS.

Report ID Theft to Law Enforcement. If your SSN was compromised and you think you may be the victim of tax-related ID theft, file a police report.

Complete an Identity Theft Affidavit.

Understand IRS Notices. Once the IRS verifies a taxpayer's identity, the agency will mail a particular letter to the taxpayer.

PINs. If a taxpayer reports that they are a victim of ID theft or the IRS identifies a taxpayer as being a victim, they will be issued a PIN

Report Suspicious Activity. If you suspect or know of an individual or business that is committing tax fraud.

Buzzing Around Tax Facts With Be's

Combating ID Theft. Over the past few years, nearly 2,000 people were convicted in connection with refund fraud related to identity theft. The average prison sentence for identity theft-related tax refund fraud grew to 43 months in 2014 from 38 months in 2013, with the longest sentence being 27 years. During 2014, the IRS stopped more than $15 billion of fraudulent refunds, including those related to identity theft.

Need Identity Theft Protection:

www.indiaroberts.legalshieldassociate.com

Tax Scams for the Filing Season

The IRS has seen a surge of these phone scams in recent months as scam artists threaten police arrest, deportation, license revocation and other things. The IRS reminds taxpayers to guard against all sorts of con games that arise during any filing season.

"If someone calls unexpectedly claiming to be from the IRS with aggressive threats if you don't pay immediately, it's a scam artist calling," said IRS Commissioner John Koskinen. "The first IRS contact with taxpayers is usually through the mail. Taxpayers have rights, and this is not how we do business."

The Dirty Dozen is compiled annually by the IRS and lists a variety of common scams taxpayers may encounter any time during the year. Many of these con games peak during filing season as people prepare their tax returns or hire someone to do so. This year for the first time, the IRS will issue the individual Dirty Dozen scams one at a time during the next 12 business days to raise consumer awareness.

Phone scams top the list this year because it has been a persistent and pervasive problem for many

Buzzing Around Tax Facts With Be's

taxpayers for many months. Scammers are able to alter caller ID numbers to make it look like the IRS is calling. They use fake names and bogus IRS badge numbers. They often leave "urgent" callback requests. They prey on the most vulnerable people, such as the elderly, newly arrived immigrants and those whose first language is not English. Scammers have been known to impersonate agents from IRS Criminal Investigation as well.

"These criminals try to scare and shock you into providing personal financial information on the spot while you are off guard," Koskinen said. "Don't be taken in and don't engage these people over the phone."

Filing Fake Documents to Hide Income

Hiding taxable income by filing false Form 1099s or other fake documents is a scam that taxpayers should always avoid and guard against, the Internal Revenue Service said today. This scheme is one of those on the annual "Dirty Dozen" list of tax scams for the 2015 filing season.

"The mere suggestion of falsifying documents to reduce tax bills or inflate tax refunds is a huge red flag when using a paid tax return preparer." said IRS Commissioner John Koskinen. "People should watch out for this type of scam especially when someone else prepares their returns."

Compiled annually, the "Dirty Dozen" lists a variety of common scams that taxpayers may encounter any time but many of these schemes peak during filing season as people prepare their returns or hire people to help with their taxes.

Illegal scams can lead to significant penalties and interest and possible criminal prosecution. IRS Criminal Investigation works closely with the

Buzzing Around Tax Facts With Be's

Department of Justice (DOJ) to shutdown scams and prosecutes the criminals behind them.

Buzzing Around Tax Facts With Be's

Thank for your support

Anee B

2016

Made in the USA
San Bernardino, CA
16 February 2016